...coming!

JOHN OSTEEN

What should you do?
The answer to your prayer has not come!
This book will explain a Bible principle
that will cause faith to triumph.

Copyright © 1980 by John Osteen

ISBN 0-912631-25-2

Lakewood Church
P.O. Box 23297
Houston, Texas 77228

BOOKS BY JOHN OSTEEN

*A Miracle For Your Marriage
*Believing God For Your Loved Ones
*Healed of Cancer *by Dodie Osteen*
*How To Claim the Benefits of the Will
*How To Demonstrate Satan's Defeat
 How To Flow in the Super Supernatural
 How to Release the Power of God
 Overcoming Hindrances to Receiving the
    Baptism in the Holy Spirit
*Overcoming Opposition: How To Succeed in
    Doing the Will of God *by Lisa Comes*
*Pulling Down Strongholds
 Reigning in Life as a King
 Rivers of Living Water
*6 Lies the Devil Uses to Destroy Marriages
    by Lisa Comes
*The Believer's #1 Need
 The Bible Way to Spiritual Power
 The Confessions of a Baptist Preacher
*The Divine Flow
*The 6th Sense...Faith
 The Truth Shall Set You Free
*There is a Miracle in Your Mouth
 This Awakening Generation

(continued next page)

Unraveling the Mystery of the Blood Covenant
*What To Do When the Tempter Comes
You Can Change Your Destiny

Minibooks

*A Place Called There
*ABC's of Faith
Deception! Recognizing True and False Ministries
Four Principles in Receiving From God
How To Minister Healing to the Sick
*How to Receive Life Eternal
Keep What God Gives
*Love & Marriage
*Receive the Holy Spirit
Saturday's Coming
Seven Facts About Prevailing Prayer
Seven Qualities of a Man of Faith
*What To Do When Nothing Seems to Work

Selected titles also available in Spanish.

Please write for a complete list of prices in the
Book and Tape Library of John Osteen. Write to:

Lakewood Church
P.O. Box 23297
Houston, Texas 77228

Saturday's Coming

John Osteen

My heart's desire is to help people everywhere in the Body of Christ. When I get through
with a meeting, if I have not helped people, my
journey has been in vain. I used to do a lot of
preaching and shouting and dancing and jump-
ing and I had a lot of good meetings. I know a lot
of good was done at the time; but when the dust
was settled and all the meetings were over and I
went to my hotel room, many times I just felt like
crying because I knew that *lasting* good was not
done. The people were too wrought up in emotion and the real work of the Word had not
taken effect in their lives. My goal is to help you.
If you will sincerely read the truths presented in
this book, meditate on the scriptures and let the
Word of God take root in your heart, God will effect great changes in your life.

Jesus in talking about faith in Mark 11:24: "Therefore I say unto you, what things soever you desire when you pray, believe that you receive them and you shall have them."

First of all, you find out what the Word of God says in regards to your family situation, your body, your mind, your emotions, your finances, your business, or whatever it is you desire. Then you pray and believe that you receive your answer. You do not believe that you *have*, you believe that you *receive*, **then** you shall have.

I want to explain to you in this book the spiritual principles to apply from the time you say with a heart full of faith, "I believe I have received," and the time you actually see the answer come into manifestation.

The time span may be a day, it may be an hour, it may be a week, it may be a year, between the time that you see the truth, believe the Word of God, receive it by reaching out with your hands of faith, receiving it in your spirit man, and the time it is actually manifested in your life. A certain amount of time may pass before "ye shall have it" comes to pass. In that period of time, what shall we do? How shall we conduct ourselves? This is the time period in which you will need to learn how to develop an unshakable confidence in Almighty God.

If there ever was a time the devil will try to shake your confidence in God and His Word, it is between the time you say, "I do now believe that I have received" and the time you see the manifestation and can say, "I have it." You do not always get things instantly! There is a time span in which you may have to wait for a manifestation. During that time you have to make up your mind whether you have any confidence in God or not. You have to decide if you have any confidence in His Word.

I John 5:14 says, "And this is the confidence that we have in Him, that, if we ask any thing according to His will, He heareth us. . . ."

God tells us that we can have confidence. In what? In Him! This is the confidence that we have in Jesus. It pleases God and it honors God for us to have confidence in Him. When He looks at you and sees you trusting totally in His Word, it thrills His heart.

I John 5:15 says, "And if we know that He hears us, whatsoever we ask, we know that we have the petitions that we desired of Him."

Even before what we have asked for manifests, we know that we have the petitions that we

7

desired of Him. That is the confidence that we have in God. If we ask anything in line with His Word, we know that He hears us. Since we know He hears us, we know that we have whatsoever we ask. We know *we have it*. Confidence is knowing we have it.

Somebody may ask you, "Do you think you have something that you can't see?"

Have you ever seen your brains?!!

The Bible tells us that we can have confidence in Him. Our faith rests in the integrity of a Person. It is not some doctrine. It is not just in something written somewhere, but our confidence is in *Him*. Our confidence says, "If He hears me, and He does; if I pray in line with the Word, I *know that I have*, He heard me and I have it."

Hebrews 10:35: "Cast not away therefore your confidence, which hath great recompense of reward."

You need to develop an unshakable confidence.

Your confidence has a *great* recompense of reward. It will save your life. It will save your business. It will save your family. It will reach out and get your child out of drugs and out of alcohol. It will straighten out your marriage.

8

"Cast not away therefore your confidence which hath *great* recompense of reward, for ye have need of patience, that after ye have done the will of God, you might receive the promise." (Hebrews 10:35, 36)

"And we desire that every one of you do shew the same diligence to the full assurance of hope unto the end." (Seek an unshakable confidence in God.) "That ye be not slothful, but followers of them who through faith and patience inherit the promises." (Hebrews 6:11, 12)

We need to seek that same confidence unto the end. Hebrews 4:1 & 2, "Let us therefore fear (or have reverence) lest, a promise being left us of entering into rest, any of you seem to come short of it. For unto us was the Gospel preached as well as unto them. But the Word preached did not profit them. . . ."

When the Word of God goes forth, it can either profit you or not profit you. It did not profit them. It was not mixed with faith.

God has given you some promises. He tells you to be reverent and cautious lest you lose a promise being left you of entering into his rest on any position — financially, materially, spiritually, maritally, or any other way. There is divine rest in every area. Let us therefore be

9

careful now lest a promise be left us that we should seem to come short of it. Dare to believe God for everything that is yours!

We need to be quick to do the Word. Faith is acting on the Word. Faith has nothing to do with emotion. Get it settled in your heart that it has nothing to do with feeling and emotion. It is simply acting like God told you the truth! Some people wait for some great manifestation of faith. They expect goosebumps or hot flashes! That is ridiculous. Faith is an act!

Faith is not an emotion. Faith is acting on a legal contract.

This truth can change your situation.

When you read a scripture that you can apply to your situation, faith grows in your heart. It's not an outward show with kicking and shaking and trembling. **No!** You can simply receive God's Word and begin to act like it is so.

Go ahead and live in the light of that scripture.

I want all the Word to profit me. Even though the Word was preached to the Israelites, it did not profit them, not being mixed with faith. It wasn't because they didn't believe it but they didn't act on it when they heard it. Hebrews 4:3 says, "For we which have believed, do enter into rest. . . ." When you believe, you enter into rest! You don't have to wring your hands and constantly say, "Bless God, I tell you, I'm a man of faith. I tell you I do believe, I do believe."

No! That is not rest. That is anxiety. That is frustration. That is stubbornness. There is a lot of difference between stubbornness and trying to prove to people that you believe something (when you don't believe it), and true faith.

Some people are trying to convince themselves. They that do believe, do enter into what? Rest!

Hebrews 4:9-10, "There remaineth therefore a rest to the people of God. For he that entered into his rest has ceased from his own works as God did from His."

Faith has a divine rest.

Faith rests. When God's Word gets down into your heart and you know that God has heard you, there is an unshakable rest. Your part is to seek God and study His Word. Study every day. Meditate on His truths until one day a sweet, divine rest engulfs you. Then you will know that everything is all right. Faith has rest. No matter how much the storm blows and the wind howls around your house, you can have rest.

Let me share with you an illustration of God's rest. There was a picture painting contest. Each entry was to illustrate peace and rest. There were

11

lots of entries. There were pastural scenes and beautiful pictures of majestic mountains. There were seascapes and sunsets. They were all so well done. But right in the midst of these tranquil scenes was a picture of a storm.

The lightning was flashing across the sky. It was so detailed, you could almost hear the thunder. The sky was black and storm clouds hung low on the horizon. There were mountains in this picture and right there in the crag of a rock, hiding from the wind, was a little mother bird with her nest safe in the rock, in the cleft of the rock. She sat there singing with all of her might while her little brood was in the nest. That is real peace. That is true rest. The divine rest that God gives is not necessarily getting to a place where you don't have any storms. Jesus' rest can be yours in the midst of the storm!

That little bird had known by instinct that all the winds of this world could not blow that mountain down! The same Creator that created safety for the bird is your Heavenly Father who will keep you safe throughout all the storms that life can bring.

From the time that you read the Word of God and you believe the Word of God; and the time that you believe you receive from God, and the time that you actually see the physical answer — the money in your hand, a child comes home, your marriage straightened out, the manifestation in your body, emotional stability, the overcoming of fear, or whatever it is you are desiring from God — you need to abide by God's principles in order to actually have what you believe you receive.

You say, "I do now receive. I may not have it in manifestation but I now receive." The time has not yet come when you actually see it, feel it and know it is yours in manifestation.

Are you waiting for a manifestation from God? Do you know it is already yours? What is it that you are to do during that time when the devil wants to shake your confidence in God? What is it that you are to do? What is your activity? What shows your unshakable confidence in God?

It is a life of praise for God's Word and God's Word alone. You can enjoy rest that simply looks up into the face of God and praises Him because you know it's yours in spite of all the devil can say to you.

The Bible says, "Whoso offereth praise, glorifieth Me: and to him that ordereth his conversation aright will I shew the salvation of God." (Psalm 50:23)

How are you to live when you believe that God has given you that desire but there is as yet

13

absolutely no manifestation? You should live a life of praise that glorifies God, that confesses the Word in joy before the Father's throne.

I have five children. (I want to say to you who are raising children, you won't die! You will live!) Thank God for children. The Bible says, "Children are an heritage of the Lord: and the fruit of the womb is His reward."

I have three daughters. They are always wanting dresses. Suppose my little girl came to me and said, "Daddy, I want a dress, I want a dress." I would say, "All right." (It is Monday.) So, I would say to her, "Darling, this is Monday, but if you will just trust me today and wait a bit, I am going to buy you that dress on Saturday." She would leap for joy because she knows she is going to get a new dress on Saturday. What does she do between Monday and Saturday? All she does is just live in joy. She pictures that new dress in her mind. She is already by faith wearing that dress. She envisions herself beautifully clothed in that dress. There is not a doubt in her mind. She tells everybody she meets about the new dress. Someone asks, "Why are you so happy?" She answers, "I'm going to have my new dress Saturday. I am getting a new dress. It's mine, it's mine, it's mine."

That person might say, "Well I don't see it."

But she knows it's hers. It will manifest on Saturday. She probably meditates on my promise every day. "I've got it. My daddy said I got the dress. I may not have it now, but it's mine."

Now why does she get happy on Monday? Why does she rejoice on Tuesday, Wednesday, Thursday, and Friday? Because she knows Saturday is coming. She knows Saturday is coming as sure as the sun rises and sets. At night she spends her time laying in bed just thinking about that dress. "Oh, I'm so glad I got my dress. I'm so glad I got my dress."

I want you to notice that I only answered her once about the dress. I merely said, "Yes." Never once did she ever come back and say, "Now Daddy, are you sure you are not lying to me?" If she had doubted my promise, she would have become downcast and depressed. Her friends would ask, "Why are you sad?" She would have to answer, "My daddy said I was going to get a dress, but you know I can't trust him. He is probably lying to me." That would be a sad situation. Thank God she will never have to say that, because she has confidence in my word. She knows it is good from Monday until Saturday. She can rejoice and live in joy and imagine wearing that dress because she knows Saturday *is* coming.

15

I remember the time in my life when I was writing the book, *There's A Miracle in Your Mouth;* I was in the greatest pain of any time in all of my life. The devil attacked my body. The devil came against me. I had muscle spasms in my back. I could hardly move without screaming. I couldn't sleep at night. I had such excruciating pain in my back, it seemed like every disc was ruptured. It seemed like every vertebrae was out of place. *Never* have I been in such pain! What a joy it is today to be without pain.

During these weeks of writing, the devil told me, "You have bad back trouble. You are going to have to have surgery. You are going to be paralyzed. You are going to be in a wheelchair. You will never live a normal life again." Many times it seemed like he was telling me the truth, because there was such pain. I couldn't rest. The devil harassed and ridiculed me. He taunted me in saying, "You are a hypocrite. While you sit here writing *There's A Miracle in Your Mouth* you are more sickly than anybody! You are not going to get well. You are a liar. You are writing lies. As soon as that book gets printed you will be in a wheelchair. You better stop writing lies and deceiving God's people. There's not a miracle in your mouth. There's not a miracle in your life. You are not well.

Why should you tell anybody else about how to get well? It's not working for you." Those were haunting lies and the chiding of the devil!!

My back was hurting. The muscle spasms were constant. Pain would cause me to almost scream out. I didn't scream out. Instead, every morning I would get up after a sleepless night. I would go outside and walk and talk to God. I would say, "Father, I praise you. I want to thank you that I have received my healing. Thank God, I have received my healing by faith. Galatians 3:13 says, 'Christ hath redeemed us from the curse of the law, being made a curse for us; for it is written, cursed is every one that hangeth on a tree.' Thank You that I did receive my healing at the very moment I asked You. I have received. I know this is just Monday. But I want to thank You that *Saturday is coming*. I am going to spend the time between now and Saturday just praising You. I praise and thank You, Father."

As I praise God and thank Him for the manifestation, I can see myself out of that situation. I can see myself delivered. I become filled with joy as I behold myself completely healed!

Doing this gives the devil a nervous breakdown! It will put him on tranquilizers! It will shake him up! As I prayed on Monday, I knew Saturday was coming. I knew that God had promised me more than a new dress. I knew that healing was mine. I did not spend my time begging and questioning God, but with an unshakable confidence in the Lord, I just praised Him, and praised Him, and praised Him. When I finished writing that book, *There's A Miracle in Your Mouth*, the devil packed his bags and took off. I have never had a bit of back trouble since that time! You see, the Bible teaches us we should live a life of praise.

Praise is faith at work.

When you say what God says about your situation, you will begin to see yourself as God sees you. When you beg God, you are letting the devil shake your confidence in the Lord. Every trial, every sickness, every trouble that comes your way is of the devil. Every trial is the effort of the devil to shake your confidence in God. When you doubt and fear, it is because we have suddenly believed the circumstance rather than God.

God says of Abraham in Romans 4:20, "He staggered not at the promise of God through unbelief; but was strong in faith, giving glory to God." He grew strong in faith, giving praise to God. You see, he praised God before he ever saw Isaac. If there had been a gynecologist in Abraham's day, he would have examined Sarah and called her "crazy." Sarah did not conceive a child for twenty-four years after God had spoken the promise. Yet, Abraham just looked up to heaven and said, "Saturday's coming! Saturday's coming! Saturday's coming!" He praised God and grew strong in faith as he looked at the Word of God and praised God that His Word could not be shaken. He had an unshakable confidence in God.

In Joshua, chapter 6, we read the story of Joshua marching around the walls of Jericho. They went around praising God and shouted **before** the walls fell down. Some people say, "Well, I tell you it's hard to praise God that I'm well when I'm sick." If God says I'm well, I don't say I'm sick! I say, "I'm well." I begin to praise God that I am well. Praise is faith at work!

Between Monday and Saturday we should praise God because the answer is on the way!

In II Chronicles 20:21-22, Jehoshaphat sent the singers out before the army and they praised the Name of the Lord. The battle was won because they began to praise the Name of the Lord.

Somebody said, "Jesus certainly would not praise God before a manifestation." The Bible says in John 11:41-42 that He stood before Lazarus' grave and simply praised God while Lazarus was still dead.

When Jesus came to Bethany, they told Him all

about it.

"When Jesus therefore saw her weeping, and the Jews also weeping which came with her, He groaned in the spirit, and was troubled, and said, "Where have ye laid him? They said unto Him, Lord, come and see. Jesus wept." (John 11:33-35)

He was so merciful and compassionate. The Jews mocked Jesus. They thought he wept for sorrow and despair. Some of them said, "Could not this man which opened the eyes of the blind, have caused that this man should not have died?" Jesus gave a groaning in Himself. (In every crowd there are some gripers, complainers and questioners.) He came to the grave which was a cave with a stone laid upon it. Jesus told them to take away the stone. Lazarus had been dead for four days.

In verse 40 Jesus said, "Did not I say if you believe you would see the glory of God?" They then took away the stone from the place where the dead laid, and Jesus lifted His eyes and said, "Father, I thank You that You *have* heard Me."

Jesus functioned in the same law that we are talking about here. He said, "Father, I thank You that You *have* (past tense) heard Me." Lazarus was still dead, but he is saying, "Father, I thank You that he is alive. I thank You that he is out of the grave." He praised God *before* Lazarus was raised from the dead.

Actually, He was saying, "Father, I thank You that You have heard Me. I have already received the answer to My prayer. I already see Lazarus raised. I thank You that You *have* heard Me."

Jesus praised the Father when there was no evidence of life. He thanked Him for already answering Him.

You are not going to be wealthy, you **are** wealthy. It is not that you are going to be well, you **are** well. It is not that you are going to be healed, you **are** healed. It is not that you are going to be victorious, you **are** victorious.

You must be able to stand in the midst of all the evidence of deadness and say, "Father, I thank You that You have heard me. I am healed. I am delivered. I have the desires of my heart." Then, turn to your circumstances and command them to line up with the Word of God.

Between Monday and Saturday, we will praise God.

Praise is faith at work!

Look at the story of Jonah 1:1-3, "Now the Word of the Lord came unto Jonah the son of Amittai, saying, Arise, go to Nineveh, that great city, and cry against it; for their wickedness is come up before me. But Jonah rose up to flee unto Tarshish from the presence of the Lord. . . ." The Word of the Lord came to Jonah and told him to go preach down at Nineveh. Instead of obeying God, he ran the other way. Have you ever run away from God? Jonah paid his passage and went on a ship. During the journey a storm began to rage. This disobedient, rebellious prophet slept during the storm. The crewman found him asleep. The storm was raging; you see, they wanted to find out why. They knew something was wrong. They tried to find out the cause of such a storm. They knew there was a reason. They began to examine. Finally they woke him up and questioned him. Soon he admitted that he was disobedient to God and the cause of the storm. He said, "I'm the rebel, I'm the one running from God. Take me and throw me overboard and you will have peace."

They picked him up and threw him overboard. But God prepared a great fish and commanded that it receive Jonah at the time they threw him overboard. That whale just opened his mouth and down went Jonah. Now Jonah found himself on the inside of that whale. As he sat there in all the slime and gastric juices and seaweed wrapped around his head, I'm sure he thought he would soon die. Yet, in the midst of all that, Jonah found deliverance.

If Jonah can get out of a whale, surely you can

get out of a whale of a lot of trouble! How did Jonah get his deliverance? Jonah 2:1 says, "Then Jonah prayed unto the Lord his God out of the fish's belly." Did you know you can pray in the whale's belly? If he could pray inside of a fish, you can certainly pray in the midst of your trouble! Jonah prayed unto the Lord out of the fish's belly and cried unto God, "And said, I cried by reason of mine affliction unto the Lord, and he heard me; out of the belly of hell cried I, and thou heardest my voice. For thou hadst cast me into the deep, in the midst of the seas; and the floods compassed me about: all thy billows and thy waves passed over me. Then I said, I am cast out of thy sight; yet I will look again toward thy holy temple. The waters compassed me about, even to the soul: the depth closed me round about, the weeds were wrapped about my head. I went down to the bottoms of the mountains; the earth with her bars was about me for ever; yet hast thou brought up my life from corruption, O Lord my God." (Jonah 2:2-6)

Notice that Jonah recalled, "When my soul fainted within me, I remembered the Lord." If you can just get your eyes on the Eternal, Almighty God that created heaven and earth, there is hope for you!

Remember God when your son has gone astray.

Remember God when your daughter has fallen by the way. Remember God when your business has failed. Remember God when the doctor says you can't live. Remember God when the situation looks dark. Jonah said, "I remembered the Lord."

Look at Jonah 2:9, "But I will sacrifice unto Thee with the voice of thanksgiving. . . ." What did Jonah do between Monday and Saturday while sitting in that fish? He offered the sacrifice of thanksgiving and praise.

Are you sitting in the whale's belly today? Does it look like Saturday will never come? What are you to do? Are you to run to every prayer line? Are you to run down the aisle every time somebody prays? Are you to cry, beg, and doubt God? Or are you to sit there and say, "Mr. Fish, you may look like you have gotten me forever, but I have remembered the Eternal God. I have His Word. Salvation is of the Lord. I know that He will get me out of this situation. I see myself out of it. As I sit here in the whale's belly, I will offer unto the Lord the sacrifice of thanksgiving and praise. Lord, I praise You that I am out of the whale's belly. I praise You, Lord, the seaweed is unwrapped from my neck. I praise you that I am out of the slime. I praise you Lord, that I am out of this terrible situation."

Think about Jonah. Consider his situation.

Everywhere he looked there was whale. Trouble surrounded him.

Somebody said, "But it is so hard to believe God when the doctor says I'm going to die." The doctor could be wrong. Everywhere Jonah looked there was whale. It was a hopeless situation for Jonah; but thanksgiving and praise touched the heart of God. All God had to do was speak to that fish and the fish instantly vomited him up. Jonah came on to dry ground running and preaching!

If Jonah could praise God in the midst of a whale, can't you praise God in the midst of some sort of a physical discomfort? Can't you praise God in spite of you seeing whale every place? Can you look up in the face of God and just praise Him with joy because you already see your child serving God, your home filled with peace and love, and the situation in your business already resolved?

This is the secret to developing an unshakable confidence in God. The devil will come and try to shake your confidence in God. Let me share with you an incident from my own life that will illustrate this truth. We used to have a convention every year during Thanksgiving at Lakewood Church. During these conventions we would serve food to the people. One particular year I determined that I was going to have faith to buy two head of cattle or that somebody would give us two head of cattle. Then we would slaughter them and have meat for all the meals. So, I stood up before our congregation and I boldly made my confession, "My God shall supply all my need. I need two head of cattle. I am setting myself in faith toward God that I will have two head of cattle that we will slaughter and the meat will be supplied for our convention."

Boldly, I made my confession. "Two cows, two cows, two cows, two cows." I made it several times, but Saturday didn't come very quickly. I waited and waited and waited and waited. The convention was getting close. There were no cows, not even one cow. No cows! There is an area where the devil can try to shake you. One day I heard a voice whisper in my ear as if someone was sitting on my shoulder and it said, "You're not going to get those cows. In fact, you know you have money in the treasury to buy cows and to buy meat and there is no use of you worrying over all of this."

I shook myself. I said, "I believe, I believe, I believe." I told the next person I met, "I believe God has supplied us some cows. We have two head of cattle. We are going to slaughter them. Meat is provided for our convention."

The truth is, though, that I had begun to get a little weak. A few days later I heard a voice saying to me, "Now why do you want to go through all of this? The time is drawing nigh. After all, you have the money and you are a busy preacher. You do not have time to bother with trying to have faith for two cows. Just buy them." I said, "Yes, I am a busy preacher. Why should I spend time worrying about two cows? After all, our faith provided the money we have, so we can just buy the cows."

So, I became quiet about it, and I decided to just go buy the meat and everybody would forget about it. I can remember the very minute that I let go of believing God for the cows. Something left out of me in my spirit. I released it. I gave up. I lost my confidence. I did not lose confidence in a doctrine or in a scripture, but in a Person.

I bought the meat. We had a great Convention. I thought I got by with it. A few days afterwards the Lord gave me a visitation in the night. In this visitation, He took me down a lonely country road. As I looked to my left, I saw the biggest snakes I have ever seen in my life. They looked forty or fifty feet long. As I walked down the lonely country road, they instantly caught my attention. The Lord had me walk up close to the snakes and gaze at them. As I got closer, I noticed that the two of them were bulging with a distinct outline of a cow. I saw the head, I saw the shoulders, I saw the backbone, I saw the hip bone. I saw it all. There was a cow in one, and a cow in the other. Then the Lord said to me, "I just wanted you to know that you let the devil swallow your cows!"

I learned a valuable lesson from this experience and the subsequent visitation from the Lord. I thank God that I only lost two cows and not my life! I am glad God let me learn on cows!

I can remember a time when the devil attacked me in my body. I could not walk in the heat. I had little physical energy. The heat would suffocate me to where I could hardly breathe. I would have to get to a cool place to breathe. That was many years ago. Recently I was in a Southern state in the heat of summer. My wife and I took a long walk outside during the hottest part of the day. As we walked along, I told my wife, "I am so happy. It is wonderful to be healed, to have strength and energy, health and joy." She turned to me and said, "We are not one bit happier now than we were when we first believed God. Even when the symptoms were present, we still believed on the Word. We are just as happy now as we were then, because we knew the answer was ours all along."

This principle of God will give you the same joy and happiness on Monday, Tuesday, Wednesday, Thursday, or Friday as you will have on Saturday! Why? Because God's answer is yours the very moment you pray and believe you receive it. It is yours!!

Every day you should praise God for what He has promised you. If it is a physical need, even if the symptoms rage in your body, do not put your attention on the symptoms. In Matthew 14:29 and 30, Peter was walking on the water and his eyes were fixed on Jesus. Did you know that the waves were just as high and the wind was just as strong when he was walking as it was when he sank? He walked because he did not look at the waves. He did not heed the wind, he looked at Jesus. But when he turned his attention to the high waves and the strong wind, he sank. Jesus is the Word of God. He is the Living Word. No matter how high the waves billow or how strong the wind may blow, do not get your attention on them. Just keep on walking, keep on walking!

Every contrary thing that comes against you financially, mentally, emotionally, morally, in your home, maritally, physically, or any contrary thing that tries to get you to doubt God's Word should be the very indication to you that you need to keep on looking at Jesus. Keep your eyes on the Word of God.

Habakkuk 3:17-19: "Although the fig tree shall not blossom" (Is your fig tree not blossoming?), . . . "neither shall fruit be in the vines; the labor of the olive shall fail, and the fields shall yield no meat; the flock be cut off from the fold, and there be no herd in the stalls: **yet** I will *rejoice* in the Lord, I will joy in the God of my salvation. The Lord God is my strength, and He will make my feet like hinds' feet, and He will make me to walk upon mine high places. . . ."

Although your fig tree may not blossom, you are rejoicing and praising God because it shall blossom. Is there no fruit in the vine? Rejoice because the fruit will come! If there is no labor in the olives, you are rejoicing because it will come. Does your field yield no meat? Rejoice because it shall yield meat. If the flocks are cut off from the fold, they shall be in the stall! Rejoice in the Lord. He is the God of your salvation. Habakkuk said that if everything looks bad, what shall you do to show your confidence in God? " . . . **Yet shall I rejoice in the Lord. I will joy in the God of my salvation.**"

How would you act if you had today what you are believing for? How would you act if today was your Saturday? What if you actually saw, felt, smelled, and touched the manifestation? How happy would you get?

This is how you should feel and act right now! As you praise God, headaches will leave you. Anxiety will fall away from your life. It may be on a Monday that God, your Heavenly Father, says that He will supply all your needs and give you the desires of your heart. It may not yet be Saturday, but Saturday's coming. All you need to do is spend your time praising the Lord. Settle it in your heart as to what your specific desire is. Then picture yourself having it and release your faith and start praising God.

You may be seeking healing and deliverance, or the help of the Lord in any area. When you praise God and rejoice in His presence, disease departs, demons flee, and the enemy is defeated. Don't think it is a burden to do this, but know that this is faith at work!

This is how you begin exercising your faith by your praise and your words of praise. Saturday will come!

Make the Following
Confession of Faith

Dear Heavenly Father, I come to You in faith believing that Your Word is true. Jesus Christ is the same yesterday, today and forever. Your Word tells me that whatsoever I desire when I pray, that if I will believe that I receive it, I shall have it. I have made my desires known to You and I do believe that I do receive my answer right now. I praise You that because I have asked according to Your will, I have the assurance in my heart that You have heard me and that You are working Your will and good pleasure in my life.

I rejoice right now that You have given me the desires of my heart. I will not be moved by circumstances and what I see with my eyes, because Your Word is true and I believe Your Word. I will rejoice and praise you every day until I actually *have* the manifestation of the answer. I thank You, Lord Jesus, that nothing is impossible to You. Right now I will begin to act my faith and I let the joy of the Lord flood my life for I believe that I have received the answers to my every prayer. Hallelujah!